Avoid
Plagiarism

SUPER
QUICK
SKILLS

Avoid Plagiarism

Thomas Lancaster

Los Angeles | London | New Delhi
Singapore | Washington DC | Melbourne

Los Angeles | London | New Delhi
Singapore | Washington DC | Melbourne

SAGE Publications Ltd
1 Oliver's Yard
55 City Road
London EC1Y 1SP

SAGE Publications Inc.
2455 Teller Road
Thousand Oaks, California 91320

SAGE Publications India Pvt Ltd
B 1/I 1 Mohan Cooperative Industrial Area
Mathura Road
New Delhi 110 044

SAGE Publications Asia-Pacific Pte Ltd
3 Church Street
#10-04 Samsung Hub
Singapore 049483

Editor: Jai Seaman
Editorial assistant: Lauren Jacobs
Production editor: Nicola Carrier
Proofreader: Emily Ayers
Marketing manager: Catherine Slinn
Cover design: Shaun Mercier
Typeset by: C&M Digitals (P) Ltd, Chennai, India
Printed in the UK

Library of Congress Control Number: 2019943992

British Library Cataloguing in Publication data

A catalogue record for this book is available from
the British Library

ISBN 978-1-5297-0497-6

At SAGE we take sustainability seriously. Most of our products are printed in the UK using responsibly
sourced papers and boards. When we print overseas we ensure sustainable papers are used as measured
by the PREPS grading system. We undertake an annual audit to monitor our sustainability.

Contents

Everything in this book!

Section 1   What do I need to know about plagiarism as a student?

Universities treat plagiarism as a serious academic issue. This section will help you to understand why.

Section 2   Why is it important for me to avoid plagiarism?

If you fail to avoid plagiarism, this will hurt your academic progress and results. In some situations, you could be removed from your course.

Section 3   What does it mean to study with integrity?

When you avoid plagiarism, you show that you're approaching your studies with integrity. You're demonstrating values such as honesty, responsibility and respect.

Section 4   When do I need to credit my sources?

You should always the credit words and ideas you use that are based on other sources and which aren't common knowledge.

Section 5   How do I credit my sources?

To credit your sources, you follow a system of referencing, allowing people to trace the words and ideas you used.

Section 6   What are some practical ways to avoid plagiarism in my writing?

Developing your study skills and an academic writing style can help you to avoid plagiarism.

Section 7   How can I use software to check my work for plagiarism?

Your university may provide you with access to software that highlights text taken from other places. This is an additional tool you can use to check for accidental plagiarism and improve your academic writing.

Section 8   Where can I get help from within my university?

There will be extra classes and support services available within your university. It's important to know what these are and to take advantage of the opportunities on offer.

Section 9   How do I know I've understood how to avoid plagiarism?

This final section helps you review everything you've discovered and check that you've developed the techniques you need to avoid plagiarism.

What do I need to know about plagiarism as a student?

10 second summary

Universities consider plagiarism a bad thing. This section will help you understand why.

60 second summary

About plagiarism

Many students find themselves accused of plagiarism because they don't really understand what the term means in practice. Plagiarism occurs when you take words or ideas from another source and use them without acknowledging the source. It doesn't matter if you did this intentionally or accidentally. It's still considered an academic offence. To not end up plagiarising, you need to credit your sources and follow academic conventions. This book is here to help you to avoid plagiarism.

What is plagiarism?

A student told us

'I got into trouble for plagiarism at my university. I didn't know I was doing anything wrong.'

Universities will tell you 'don't plagiarise'. But, it's complex. They assume you know what **plagiarism** is and why it's wrong.

At university, plagiarism is considered a bad thing. It's a form of stealing. Not stealing something physical, but stealing other people's work. Stealing words and ideas; taking their intellectual property.

Plagiarism When words, information or ideas are taken from a source and used without acknowledgement, this is known as plagiarism.

What does plagiarism mean, in a university setting?

Plagiarism occurs when you use content created by someone else without following academic conventions and without attributing the **source** of that content. That content might include words, images or even ideas, to give just a few examples of what content means.

Source This refers to the source of words, ideas or other information used in your assignment, if they were not ones that you came up with.

Often, plagiarism also represents a breach of **copyright**. Although legal definitions of copyright differ by country, people own the words they produce. In a commercial setting, if you pretend you wrote something but really plagiarised it, you could be breaking the law.

Copyright Relates to the ownership of information produced.

Plagiarism doesn't have to be intentional. So, poor scholarship isn't a good reason for plagiarising. That makes sense, as it would be hard for a university to know if you intended to plagiarise or not.

Plagiarism fact

The word plagiarism comes from the Latin form 'plagiarius'. It means kidnap. So, if you plagiarise, it's as if you're kidnapping from someone. That is, if you speak Latin.

What does plagiarism mean, in practice?

If you're accused of plagiarism, it usually means that the work you've handed in is very similar to something else.

Let's think about an example of how this could happen.

You're working hard, it's late at night and you're trying to finish an essay due the next day.

You search the web for some information you need. There, you find a paragraph of perfectly written text which you copy into your essay. You mean to go back and change it, but you forget.

The end result is plagiarism. The words in your essay are not your own.

It is an easy mistake to make, but one you have to avoid. Universities think of plagiarism as a form of cheating, whether it was intentional or not. They take cases of plagiarism very seriously.

What's another example of plagiarism?

You're working on an **assignment** with another member of your class. The assignment is challenging, so you talk about the problem and find some useful websites that will help you with your writing.

> **Assignment** A piece of work undertaken as part of a course of study.

You then develop a plan for the finished assignment together. A series of points, in order, that you're both going to make.

You then share the plan, but sit down and write the assignment separately.

Sometime later, you're summoned to a university meeting to discuss plagiarism.

You both ended up making the same points in your assignments and you made them in the same order. Even some of the words were the same, as you used the points from the plan to form your subheadings.

Think back to the definition of plagiarism. It includes both **words and ideas.** Even though it wasn't intentional, both you and your classmate committed plagiarism.

When you work too closely with another student, the end result is known as collusion. Generally, universities are happy for you to discuss your approach to an assignment with other students, but they don't like you sharing any materials.

Collusion This takes place when two or more students work so closely together that the assignments they submitted show substantial similarity. It is a type of plagiarism.

Collusion

How far you can **collaborate** with other students varies from subject to subject. If you're not sure what's acceptable for your subject, it's perfectly fine for you to ask one of your instructors for advice.

Collaborate This refers to the process of working with other students during the production of an assignment.

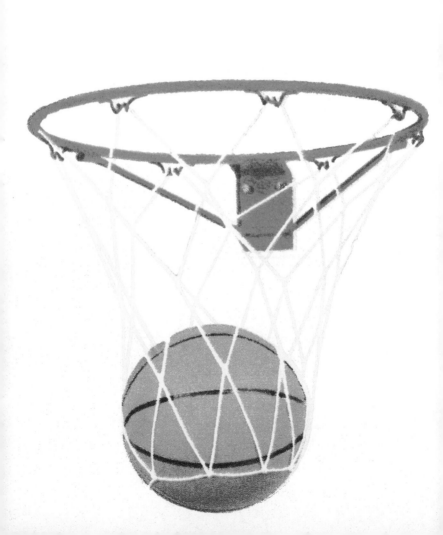

What is this book about?

This book is here to help stop you from becoming an accidental plagiarist.

The focus of this book is on written work. That is, it's there to show you how to avoid plagiarism when you write things such as essays, reports and dissertations.

Plagiarism doesn't just take place with written work. It's possible to plagiarise music, computer code, fashionable hat designs, dance sequences and even comic books. Whatever subject you're doing, keep in mind the general principle that other people own the designs, layouts and ideas they've created.

The general principles in this book apply equally to other subjects. You need to give credit where it is due. But the examples in the book will focus mainly on written work.

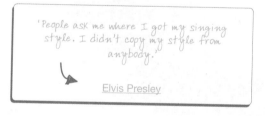

'People ask me where I got my singing style. I didn't copy my style from anybody.'

Elvis Presley

How confident are you already that you can avoid plagiarism?

Try scoring these questions on a scale of 0–5, where zero is low and five is high.

I remember plagiarism being discussed in
class and I paid attention. ☐

I know what plagiarism looks like in my academic subject. ☐

I feel confident I could discuss plagiarism with
my instructor and other students. ☐

I am proficient with the academic referencing conventions
to show when I have used other sources in my work. ☐

I know where I could turn to for help avoiding plagiarism
within my university. ☐

What is your total score for your confidence in
avoiding plagiarism? ☐

If the score is not as high as you'd like, don't worry. That's why this book is here to help you.

If you scored highly, well done. You're on your way to avoiding plagiarism. Keep reading to pick up some more tips and tricks you might not have thought about before.

Why is it important for me to avoid plagiarism?

10 second summary

Plagiarism at university has consequences in the form of academic
penalties. Plagiarism in a business
setting can be much more damaging.

60 second summary

Plagiarism has consequences

In a university setting, if you're found to have plagiarised, you're likely to receive an academic penalty. This can lead to you having to retake assignments, or even stop you from graduating. This is reflective of the real world, where plagiarism can be damaging to companies and individuals. They may have to withdraw products or pay compensation. Plagiarism can also bring them reputational damage. As a new employee, you'd be expected to understand what plagiarism is and to do your part to avoid bringing the company you're working for into disrepute.

What are the academic consequences of plagiarism?

Simply put, if you are found to have plagiarised in a university or other academic setting, you'll receive some form of penalty.

It might be relatively light, such as having to retake an assignment. You might have to take alternative subjects or study extra modules. In severe cases, you might end up being removed from your course.

Those are the immediate consequences. But the long-term effect of this could be much harder hitting.

If you are delayed from completing your course, this is going to have a financial impact on you. You might have to pay for an additional period of study. You'll have to cover your living costs. You might also delay yourself from taking graduate level employment.

You might also find that the plagiarism is recorded on your university record. This could show up in a reference if an employer asks about it. Right or wrong, employers often equate plagiarism with dishonesty, even if you didn't plagiarise intentionally.

The good news is that many universities will treat first offences lightly and not disclose these, so long as you don't reoffend. But it's best not to end up in that situation in the first place.

A student told us

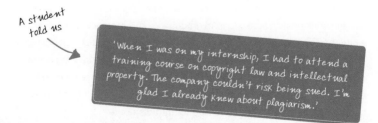

'When I was on my internship, I had to attend a training course on copyright law and intellectual property. The company couldn't risk being sued. I'm glad I already knew about plagiarism.'

What are the wider consequences of plagiarism?

Employers take plagiarism seriously because it has real effects in the outside world.

Here's an example.

Author A releases a new book. It sells well and develops a following.

A few weeks later, Author B claims that Author A has plagiarised them. The book wasn't a big seller, but it is on the same subject and they can show that some of the pages are the same.

Author A (or their publisher) is forced to withdraw their book from sale. That comes at a huge financial cost, considering all the money that has already been spent on marketing and distributing the book.

Even worse for them, Author B demands payment for the use of their intellectual property. A costly legal process ensues.

Author A is blacklisted and doesn't get work in the field again.

Think that unlikely? It's a real situation that happens all too often.

And, legal responses to plagiarism are not reserved for text. Many photographers take unauthorised use of their photos on websites very seriously, for example, and send out requests for payment. There are many forms of plagiarism in a real world setting.

'A photograph is usually looked at – seldom looked into.'

Ansel Adams

How to understand real world plagiarism

Find a recent news story involving a real world plagiarism case. You can use any news search engine you're familiar with. A popular one is Google News.

Search for 'plagiarism', find a story that looks interesting and answer the following questions.

Who are the parties involved?

....

....

....

What is it that's been plagiarised?

....

....

....

What makes this case into a form of plagiarism?

(Check back to Section 1 if you're not sure.)

....

....

....

What are the likely consequences for the party accused of plagiarism?

....

What are the likely consequences for the party whose property has been plagiarised?

....

....

....

....

Remember!

The consequences of plagiarism in the real world can be financial, or they could lead to a loss of reputation.

Have you…

Thought about what would happen if you were
found to have plagiarised within your university?......................Yes/No

Considered how this would affect your future employment? .....Yes/No

Worked out what would happen if similar
plagiarism occurred in a business situation?..............................Yes/No

Considered how you'd feel if someone plagiarised
from your work and effort? ....Yes/No

What does it mean to study with integrity?

10 second
summary

When you avoid plagiarism, you're instead showcasing yourself as having positive values. This is called operating with academic integrity.

60 second
summary

Academic integrity

There is a lot of focus at university about what plagiarism is and why this is wrong. That's quite right, as plagiarism means you're taking credit for something you don't deserve. There's also a positive side to avoiding plagiarism. When you do this, you show you're acting with the values of integrity. You're developing your abilities and your learning in a way that's ethical and above board. That's a great thing in a university situation (you're setting yourself up to get more marks), but those skills are equally valued when you complete your course and go into a professional work environment. Companies want their employees to act ethically and to demonstrate integrity.

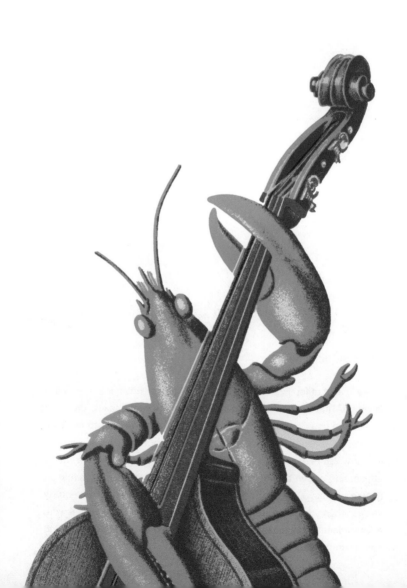

What is an alternative way of thinking about plagiarism?

So far, this book has focused on plagiarism as a negative concept. Well, that's because the whole concept is negative. Plagiarism is a form of stealing. It's taking things that don't belong to you.

Avoiding plagiarism can only be a good thing.

But there's a whole alternative way of thinking about avoiding plagiarism that's worth knowing about. By not plagiarising, you're showing that you are studying with integrity.

Integrity is important, but it is a hard concept to define. It means different things to different people.

How to define integrity

Take a look at the word chart below. It shows 15 words that you might associate with integrity in an educational setting.

Circle the five words that best represent integrity to you.

There's also blank space if you want to add extra words of your own.

Ethical	Authentic
Open	Lawful
Trustworthy	Honest
Fair	Noble
Sincere	Moral
Respectful	Leading
Uncompromising	Righteous
Principled	

....

....

'Real integrity is doing the right thing, knowing that nobody's going to know whether you did it or not.'

Oprah Winfrey

A student
told us

'To me, integrity means working to the best of my
potential inside university and beyond.'

How does academic integrity get defined?

The International Center for Academic Integrity (it's spelled 'Center' as it originated in the United States) was set up in 1992 to help universities, instructors and students think more about integrity.

To them, **academic integrity** is defined based around what they call six fundamental values.

Academic integrity means acting with:

> **Academic integrity**
> The values or shared principles you should display when writing and throughout your academic career.

1   Honesty

2   Trust

3   Fairness

4   Respect

5   Responsibility

6   Courage

These are the values you should display throughout your academic career and beyond. When thinking about avoiding plagiarism, most of these values are self-explanatory. When you write in your own words and credit your sources, you are working with fairness and honesty, showing that you can be trusted. You are demonstrating the ability to write, and taking the associated responsibility. You are showing respect for the educational system.

The value of courage is an important one. Sometimes, it's difficult to do what's right.

Let's imagine that other students in your class are plagiarising. What should you do in that situation?

Most importantly, you should continue to act with academic integrity yourself. Make sure that you don't plagiarise.

If you have courage, you might also talk to them and find out why they are plagiarising. Is it a mistake? Share with them the techniques you know about from this book (or encourage them to get their own copy; it will help them in the long run).

You might also want to discuss this with your instructor. If they're unaware that students are plagiarising, they might not know they need to put extra support in place.

But it takes courage to think beyond yourself and take action. That's what academic integrity is all about.

Understanding the values of academic integrity

You are working on an assignment and go online to look for help. You find such a good answer to the assignment online you're tempted to just download it, edit it and hand it in.

Which of the fundamental values of academic integrity would you be breaching and how?

▢ Honesty ....

▢ Trust ....

▢ Fairness ....

▢ Respect ....

▢ Responsibility ....

▢ Courage ....

Remember!

There are always temptations out there, but if you were to hand this assignment in, even if you changed it a bit, that would be a serious case of plagiarism. Not something you want to be associated with and not something you want to have on your academic record.

Congratulations

You now know what plagiarism is and how you're demonstrating integrity when you avoid plagiarism.

When do I need to credit my sources?

10 second
summary

You need to credit words you copy from other sources and the traceable ideas you use.

Giving credit

To avoid plagiarism, you need to respect your sources. That means providing credit to the originating author of the words and ideas you use. The only exception is where you're using such a fundamental idea that it would be considered as common knowledge. For instance, you wouldn't need to reference the idea that water boils at 100 degrees Celsius. If you're not sure if something is considered common knowledge or not, the best advice is to reference it anyway. It is better to be safe than sorry.

When don't I need to credit my sources?

There's a simple rule of thumb to avoid plagiarism. It's that you always need to give credit to the sources you've used. There are two main exceptions.

The first exception is when something is considered **common knowledge**. Some examples of common knowledge include:

- January has 31 days

- Scotland is part of the United Kingdom

- Vegetarians don't eat meat or fish

- Charles Dickens was an author.

The second exception is when you're talking about your **personal experience**. This is one way you can add value to your writing, particularly if you're writing a reflective account.

If you're not sure, include the expected credit. It's better to cite too much than too little.

Can I plagiarise from myself?

You can! This is known as **self plagiarism.**

Self plagiarism happens when you reuse material you've written before without permission or acknowledgement of the previous time you used it.

One way it can happen is if you're given a choice of topics to write about. Then, you end up choosing to write about very similar topics for two different assignments.

By committing self plagiarism, you'd be getting credit twice, but only doing the work once. That's why it's not allowed.

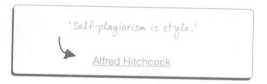

'Self-plagiarism is style.'

Alfred Hitchcock

Why should I use sources?

Using sources adds value to your work. It shows you understand the wider context surrounding your subject.

Some students think that using sources is a weakness and that instructors only want to see their new ideas.

That's not the case. By crediting your sources, showing you respect them, then building upon them, you're actually setting yourself up to get a better mark than you would by ignoring sources (or, worse still, plagiarising from them).

A student told us

'I found it's okay to cite the same source more than once in an essay.'

Think about an assignment you're working on (or one you worked on recently).

In the spaces provided below, give an example of one idea you would mention in that assignment which would be considered common knowledge relating to that topic. Then give an example of a key source for that assignment which you would have to reference.

Common knowledge

....

....

....

Key source

....

....

....

How do I credit
my sources?

10 second
summary

**To credit your sources you need
to be familiar with the referencing
system used by your university.**

60 second summary

Referencing

Referencing is a core skill needed for success in an academic environment. By referencing, you are crediting the source of the information you've used to enhance your work. There are many different referencing formats and you need to find out the one your university requires you to use. Generally, there are two components to successful referencing. First, you need to include a short citation in the text to indicate where you've relied on an external source. Second, you'll include a more detailed reference in a full reference list at the end of the document. This entry shows people reading your work where they can find that more detailed source.

How do I write reference information?

Now you know when you should reference information, it's time for a quick overview of how to reference. For a fuller guide, take a look at the Super Quick Skills *Cite Your Source* volume and the information provided by your university.

The first thing you need to be aware of is that there are many different **referencing** systems. The principles of referencing are the same, but there are some differences in the way you present the references. Take some time to find out what referencing system you should be using. This can differ from university to

Referencing The process through which the sources of information in an assignment are acknowledged.

university and from department to department. Sometimes different instructors on the same course can request different referencing formats.

There are two main parts to referencing. These are a **citation** and an entry in the **reference list**.

- **Citation** – a short entry which goes in your main text where you've used information from a source

- **Reference list** – one record for each unique source you've used. This gives detail about where someone else can find each source you used.

It's quite common to refer to the same source multiple times in a single essay. In that case, every time you refer to the source, you add a citation. But you only give the detailed information about where to find the source once in the reference list.

A student told us

'I used to find referencing confusing, but it's really very easy. You just have to follow a format.'

What's an example of writing a reference in the Harvard referencing format?

Harvard referencing is a popular format that's often used in universities (and in academic research papers).

There are lots of things you might want to reference, such as academic journal papers, lecture slides or even posts on social media. But let's say you want to write about a technique you've read in another book in the Super Quick Skills series, *Manage Your Money* by Bob Smale.

Here is a quote from the original book:

> 'If you live in shared accommodation you might develop a cooking rota so that you don't have to cook every day.'

You could use that exact quote with a citation, but a better approach would be to write around this and use your own words, still with a citation.

This would give you something like:

> One way to save money as a student is to eat with your housemates and cook in bulk. Smale (2019) recommends you put together a rota and share the cooking.

In the reference list at the end of your document, you would include:

Smale, B. (2019), Manage Your Money, Sage Publications, London, United Kingdom.

There are some slight variants in Harvard referencing formats, but this will show you the general idea.

'Quote me as saying I was mis-quoted.'

Groucho Marx

How to write about this book

It's time to practise writing about this book and, at the same time, avoiding plagiarism.

Pick a page you've read already and find a point or paragraph that you found interesting and want to write about.

Then follow the worksheet below to write a sentence, which should be in your own words, about that point, along with a citation and a reference.

The point I found interesting is

....

....

....

It is on page number

....

My university uses this referencing system:

....

....

....

They have information about how to reference available here:

....

....

Here is a sentence about the point I found interesting, written in my own words:

....

....

....

The citation in the referencing system I'm using looks like this:

....

....

....

The reference for the reference list looks like this:

....

....

....

Now you've understood the basics of referencing!

How do I use referencing software?

Software is available to help you with referencing. Some software is paid-for, some free. Your university might have a preferred reference manager or might have an agreement to provide you with access to free software.

Referencing software does the same thing as you would do manually, but helps to automate some of the process. You still have to feed it the right information and make sure that the referencing system chosen is set to meet your university requirements.

It is worth taking the time to learn referencing and practising how to reference manually. That way, you know if the software you're using is getting it right or not.

Referencing software is most useful when you're writing very long documents, or if you're using the same sources repeatedly across lots of different assignments. For short essays and reports, learning the ins and outs of the referencing software may well take you longer than just doing this by hand.

You may find services on the Internet advertising themselves as referencing generators or providing free referencing software. Treat these with care, as much of this software has links with **contract cheating** services. These are companies who say they will write your assignments for you, a clear breach of academic integrity.

Contract cheating
This occurs when you get someone else to complete an assignment for you.

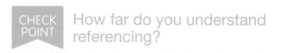

Have you found out which referencing system is used on your course?...Yes/No

Do you know what is a citation is and where to use it?..............Yes/No

Do you know what goes into a reference list?........................Yes/No

If you want to know more about referencing, check out Super Quick Skills, *Cite Your Source*.

Congratulations

You now know which sources you should identify and how to cite and reference those sources.

What are some practical ways to avoid plagiarism in my writing?

10 second summary

A lot of the time plagiarism can be accidental or caused by poor study skills. This section gives practical tips to help you to avoid plagiarism.

60 second summary

Practical tips

If you want to avoid plagiarism, it's a good idea to start working on your assignment early and to do so slowly and methodologically. Find good sources and take care to extract the right information. Then compile information from these sources into a structured assignment. By always using your own words and by citing and referencing everything as you go along, you should be able to avoid accidental plagiarism. Now, you can spend your time concentrating on making sure everything you've done is written in an appropriate academic style and that your arguments flow and make sense, all essential tools for success in an academic setting.

A student told us

'I think I know what plagiarism is, but when it comes down to it, I always end up rushing. I know I need to start working earlier and check my work much more carefully.'

How can I write better?

Academic writing is a core skill you need to master to be successful at university. Often, the very first impression someone has about your work is based on the quality of the writing. That's before they drill down into the content to make sure that everything makes sense.

> Academic writing
> The process of writing in a scholarly way, following the norms and conventions for your particular field.

If you feel confident as a writer, you're less likely to accidentally plagiarise.

Do spend some time learning academic writing skills and do take advantage of the courses and support offered by your university.

What are some tips to avoid plagiarism?

Here are some practical tips you can use to avoid accidental plagiarism. Yes, some of these are obvious, but they relate to mistakes students make all the time.

- **Manage your time well**

  Plagiarism can happen when you're tired or rushing. Work out when your best working hours are and put the effort in to draft your document well in advance of your deadlines. It's always better to have something completed, even if it's not perfect.

- **Find and evaluate more sources than you think you'll need**

  Finding good information takes time. You want to read deeply into sources, not just look at the abstracts. You might not be able to access all of the sources you want straight away. You might come up with new ideas as you complete your reading. Leave plenty of time to explore your topic before you begin writing. You'll probably find you end up reading several times more sources than you eventually use in your finished assignment.

- **Don't copy and paste from sources**

  Read the source, extract the most relevant information, then write your own version in your document. Remember, just a few words together that are the same as the source counts as plagiarism.

- **Plagiarism doesn't just refer to text**

  Maybe you've read a source and seen a great diagram or image. Generally, you should avoid reusing images as there are all kinds of copyright implications. What you can do is draw out a new version of the image, perhaps putting your own spin on it. You still need to reference the original source.

- Use quotation marks if you copy

    Sometimes, it's good to use the exact words an original author used. If you want to do this, put the text inside quotation marks and remember to reference. But keep these quotes short, no more than a sentence or two. You are trying to add value to sources, not just repeat them.

- Include your own spin on your sources

    When you read a source, it will be presented in a way that relates to whatever the original authors of that source wanted to demonstrate. But your assignment might have a different focus. When you work with information from the source, you need to relate it to your topic. You can pick and choose which bit of the source you use and include different examples.

- Reference your sources straight away

    As soon as you use information from a source in your work, add the citation to it and add the reference to your reference list. Don't intend to go back and do this afterwards. It's easy to forget.

- Check your referencing carefully

    Finish your work in good time and put it to one side for at least 24 hours. Then go back and check the document carefully. Are all the references complete and in the format required for your assignment? Are citations used wherever your assignment relates to your source? Are there any sections you're worried might be plagiarised? If so, you have time left to find better ways to word these sections.

- Take advantage of the help and support available to you in your university

    As you learn to write, your university will have help and support available for you to use. Take advantage of it. If someone will read your work and give you feedback, make sure you book an appointment. If you're worried you might have accidentally plagiarised, tell them. If you don't use the support available, you lose it.

What one thing are you going to do differently for your next assignment to improve its quality and avoid accidentally plagiarising?

....

....

....

....

'You can write rhymes but you can't write mine.'

Lin-Manuel Miranda in Hamilton:
An American Musical

How can I use software to check my work for plagiarism?

10 second
summary

There is software available that
will check your work and indicate
areas that are similar to other
sources the software knows about.

60 second summary

Software support

Software to check your work for plagiarism would be very useful, but that type of software doesn't actually exist. What does exist is software that will check your work for similarity with other sources that the software knows about. That includes web pages you might have used, academic research papers and work by other students. You should still take measures to avoid intentional plagiarism, but this software can be useful to make sure that you haven't plagiarised accidentally. Just remember that this software checks for similarity and only provides an indication. You still have to interpret the report produced by the software carefully.

What software can I use to check for plagiarism?

Many companies offer software that they advertise can be used to detect plagiarism. Some of it is aimed at universities, some at students. Your university may subscribe to one or more of these services.

This is often called plagiarism detection software, but a better name would be originality checking software or similarity checking software.

What the software will do is mark up areas of your work that are similar to sources the software knows about. Those sources might be web pages, papers from academic journals, the work of other students on your course or the work from students in previous years. Those are just a few examples.

But all the software does is mark up the documents with areas for a human to check. It doesn't say if the work is plagiarised or not.

You can ask your university if you can access this software. But that access might be limited or monitored. You might need help from an instructor to interpret the report.

What does a similarity report look like?

The similarity report will show your document, but with sections marked up, usually in different colours. These colour-coded sections show where the software thinks your words are close to those in a source it knows about.

If you've quoted and referenced everything correctly in those colour-coded sections, that should be fine. If not, you've got more work to do to avoid plagiarism.

A student told us

'My university lets us check the similarity in our work once per assignment. I'm always very careful but seeing the results after running my assignment through the software makes me confident I haven't accidentally forgotten to quote something.'

How accurate are the results from software used to check for plagiarism?

The results of using the software only give an indication of similarity, not proof of plagiarism. The results are just there as a tool to help you. The report generated is only as good as the database of sources the software has access to. So, often the software will underestimate the real extent of similarity.

The software may flag up quotes that you've referenced perfectly. That's fine. That is similarity, but it's acceptable similarity.

If you end up with a very high similarity score, but everything is quoted, you might want to look at your work again. Perhaps you've used too many quotes and not added enough of your own spin on things.

There could also be a source added to the database after you've submitted your draft. An example would be if another student on your course later handed in the same work as you. You wouldn't know about it from the similarity report, but that plagiarism would still get picked up by an instructor. Don't be tempted to copy from another student.

If you've deliberately taken a section of a paper from a source the software doesn't know about and put it in your assignment, that's still plagiarism.

What similarity score should I aim for?

There's no magic number. There's no plagiarism threshold that you should aim to get below.

Remember, similarity is okay. Plagiarism is wrong.

One of the biggest mistakes that students make is trying to get a really low similarity score, or to keep changing words until the score drops. There should always be some similarity in the documents. You will use common words and phrases whether you intend to or not.

'Words are like weapons; they wound sometimes.'

Cher

What other types of software are used to detect breaches of academic integrity?

Some of the major companies in the plagiarism detection space have begun to work on a new kind of software that tracks the writing style of documents.

Everyone has a unique style. You can see yours in the type of words you use and how complicated the vocabulary in the sentences is.

The software flags when your writing appears to be written in a different style from the one you usually use. It isn't fool proof, but it is a strong indication that someone other than you wrote the document.

So, if you're tempted to get someone else to write your assignments, don't. It's the type of activity that can get you very quickly removed from a course.

Can I use plagiarism detection software I find advertised on the Internet?

If you use software that isn't supplied by your university, you're putting yourself at risk. There are all kinds of scams out there and the software won't have access to the same database of work that the university supplied software has.

One of the biggest scams works like this:

The software is advertised as free, but there's a term hidden away in the small print. This says that, in return for checking your work, the company behind the software now owns it. They can sell it and they can republish it on their website.

If you use software like this, you could later be flagged as having plagiarised something you originally wrote. It's not worth the risk.

CHECK POINT Using software

Answer the following questions.

Does your university provide access to software
to check for possible plagiarism?....................................Yes/No

If so, what piece of software?

....

On a scale of 1 (not confident) to 10 (very confident),
how confident are you that you can interpret a report
from this type of software?

Where can I get help from within my university?

10 second summary

You will always have questions about specific assignments. This section discusses appropriate places where you can get help.

60 second
summary

Getting help

You're bound to need help during your studies. A lot of questions surrounding plagiarism are not easy ones to answer. Your university will have support available to help you, ranging from a personal tutor, to instructors, to specific services that can check your work and help improve your academic writing. You can also take extra central classes to give yourself a step up. Be careful if you're thinking about using external services. These might make so many changes to your work that what you're submitting is, in itself, a form of plagiarism. Always declare any external help and seek advice from your university if you're not sure what is appropriate.

What are the best places to go to for help?

Every university is structured differently, but they will have places you can go to for help.

Here are some common places.

Personal tutor

If you feel you're struggling due to issues outside your control, this is the person to see. There might have been an incident which means that you can't complete your assignment on time. Don't be tempted to plagiarise. Talk instead to your personal tutor; they have your best interests at heart. And, even if the personal tutor isn't the right person to help you, they will know who is.

Instructors

These are the people teaching you and responsible for the provision of specific topics. These are the people to talk to if you need clarification about what's expected from a particular assignment, or if you want to check you're working on your assignment in the right way. It's always worth contacting them if you're not sure. If you have a question, chances are that other students have one too. But don't leave this until the last minute, as you need time to put whatever advice your instructors give you into practice.

Academic support services

This might be billed as a Centre for Academic Success or for Academic Writing. This might even be part of the library. These are the people who will help you with specific questions relating to developing academic skills. They will often sit down and check your work with you. Feel free to ask them specific questions or to focus on certain areas in your assignment that are giving you trouble. They won't do your work for you, but they will flag for you areas in which you need to pay more attention.

Central university classes

You will be able to sign up for other classes which are equally useful. They might cover areas such as finding academic research papers, specific referencing systems used by your university, research skills and academic writing skills. These are really useful as they provide information beyond this book and allow you to ask questions. You can also find out what the most important information is for your university and your academic subject.

A student told us

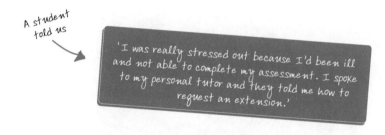

'I was really stressed out because I'd been ill and not able to complete my assessment. I spoke to my personal tutor and they told me how to request an extension.'

When can I use help outside my university?

The quick answer is to use the support services within your university first.

Yes, other services do exist which say they will proofread or edit your work. But there's no guarantee about the legitimacy of those services. Some of them are actually fronts for contract cheating services. These are companies that say they will write and produce your assignments as if they were you. Be under no illusions. This is also a form of plagiarism and a very clear type of cheating.

You've probably seen companies like that advertising before. They're everywhere. Once these companies have your contact details, they'll keep making offers to you in the hope that you cave in and buy an assignment from them.

If you do use an external service, or ask a friend to proofread your work, make sure that you indicate this on your assignment. You should keep a copy of the work from before it was edited in case you're asked for this. But, generally, good external services shouldn't change your work at all. They should only indicate areas that you should look at again, or where the wording may be unclear.

Some universities have arrangements with specific external companies and individuals that have agreed to operate within an **ethical** code of conduct. You should check if your university has such agreements in place, rather than just relying on a random name you've seen promoting themselves on the Internet.

Ethics Systems of moral principles, often thought of as separating right from wrong.

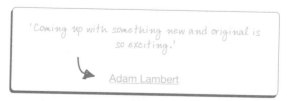

'Coming up with something new and original is so exciting.'

Adam Lambert

Do you know where you can get help from within your university?

Write down the contact details (names or websites) for the appropriate people and services available at your institution below:

Help with personal problems that are preventing you from completing your assignment

....

....

....

Support with general classes on academic writing and referencing

....

....

....

Help with checking your work for spelling mistakes and other small errors

....

....

....

Congratulations

You're not on your own! You know how you can use software to avoid accidental plagiarism and how you can get help within your university.

How do I know I've understood how to avoid plagiarism?

10 second
summary

This book has provided you with the tools you need to avoid plagiarism. This section gives you the opportunity to review everything you've found out.

60 second summary

Check your understanding

Now it's time to review everything you've read in *Avoid Plagiarism*. You need to bring together a lot of skills to do this and to show that you're equipped for success at university. These include understanding what plagiarism means and how to write while demonstrating academic integrity. You need to cite and reference information using appropriate formats. You also have to work carefully, taking time to produce the best work you can. This section brings this guide to a close before a final checklist that's there to make sure you understand everything you've found out inside *Avoid Plagiarism*.

Does plagiarism matter then?

Well done, you've made it!

Plagiarism seems like it's an easy topic to understand, but there are all kinds of places where things can go wrong.

The consequences of plagiarism are huge. You can end up failing your course, having to retake, or in some cases, you may have to leave without a qualification.

If you're working in a group and one person plagiarises, everyone in the room can end up being held equally responsible.

Luckily, you now have the tools to avoid plagiarism.

How to find out more about avoiding
plagiarism

This Super Quick Skills book has given you the skills to avoid plagiarism, but it is only a short guide. There's always more you can discover. It's time to put your new skills into practice.

Here are five questions you might be asked by another student wanting to know more about plagiarism and how to avoid it. For each question, how would you answer them?

You should be able to answer some of these questions based on information in the book and your own experience. For others, you'll have to look online and do your own research.

Remember, to avoid plagiarism, you'll need to:

- Answer the question in your own words

- Provide the source you used for information.

Question 1

'I want to use a diagram I found online as part of my assignment. Is that plagiarism? What should I do to avoid plagiarism in this case?'

My answer

....

....

....

....

The source I used

....

....

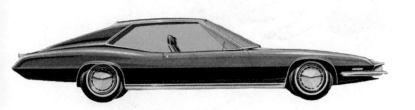

'My friend is a journalist and says that the media plagiarises all the time. Is that true? And, if it is, why should I care about avoiding plagiarism?'

My answer

. . . .

. . . .

. . . .

. . . .

The source I used

. . . .

. . . .

Question 3

'I've come across a site online that tells me I can avoid being caught plagiarising by pasting the text into my document as a picture instead of words. Does that work and what's to stop me doing this if I'll get away with it?'

My answer

. . . .

. . . .

. . . .

. . . .

The source I used

. . . .

. . . .

Question 4

'I found an essay written by another student in German and ran it through translation software to turn it into English. How do I use the translation and avoid plagiarism?'

My answer

. . . .

. . . .

. . . .

. . . .

The source I used

. . . .

. . . .

Question 5

'I saw an advert that says they'll write my report for me and it will be 100% plagiarism free. How true is that? Surely if someone else writes it for me, it's really 100% plagiarism?'

My answer

. . . .

. . . .

. . . .

The source I used

. . . .

. . . .

Some of those questions were tricky, but that's because there are ways in which plagiarism can trip you up. Well done for finding the answers!

How do I know if I've got it all together?

Avoiding plagiarism requires you to plan your work carefully, work with sources, write in your own words and acknowledge where you got the information you used from. These are core skills needed for success at university and you will produce better assignments since you have these skills. But remember, everything takes practice and you can seek help from within your university when you need it. Now work through the final checklist below to make sure you've covered and understood everything in *Avoid Plagiarism*.

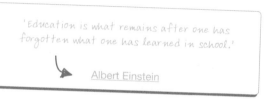

'Education is what remains after one has forgotten what one has learned in school.'

Albert Einstein

Final checklist: How to know you are done

If you've worked through this book, you'll be in a good position to avoid plagiarism.

To be sure, here is a final checklist.

Have you:

1 Considered what you need to know to
   avoid plagiarism at university?..................................Yes/No

2 Appreciated why it is important for you to avoid plagiarism?....Yes/No

3 Identified the principles of academic integrity
   that are most important for you?..................................Yes/No

4 Understood which sources you need to reference
   in your work and why?..Yes/No

5 Written citations and references in the format
   required by your university?......................................Yes/No

6   Applied some practical techniques to avoid
plagiarism in your writing?...Yes/No

7   Found out if you can access software to check
your work for accidental plagiarism?...............................Yes/No

8   Remembered that you can access further help and advice?.....Yes/No

Now it's time to make an action plan of whatever you still need to do to avoid plagiarism during your studies!

Glossary

Academic integrity   The values or shared principles you should display when writing and throughout your academic career. Some common academic integrity values include honesty, trust, fairness, respect, responsibility, and courage. By demonstrating academic integrity, you are showing a commitment to avoiding plagiarism.

Academic writing   The process of writing in a scholarly way, following the norms and conventions for your particular field. Usually, this will involve writing in a formal style and building an argument based on previous work, with the ideas from that previous work being correctly referenced.

Assignment   A piece of work undertaken as part of a course of study. This often carries marks towards a final grade but an assignment can provide feedback only. An assignment forms part of the wider assessment process. One common type of assignment is an essay, but there are many others.

Citation   A link to a source placed inside the body of an assignment. This shows where a quote or other information has been taken from that source. It provides the credit necessary to avoid plagiarism. The citation is generally a short link. More details about the source can be found in the associated reference list.

Collaborate   This refers to the process of working with other students during the production of an assignment. Some assignments may require this, for instance when they're undertaken in a group. For individual work, collaboration needs to be approached with care as working too closely with other students can lead to plagiarism.

Collusion   This takes place when two or more students work so closely together that the assignments they submitted show substantial similarity. It is a type of plagiarism.

Contract cheating   This occurs when you get someone else to complete an assignment for you. It is a form of plagiarism, since the work you hand in would not be your own. Some universities consider attempting to contract cheat, for example by asking other people to do your work, to be an academic offence.

Copyright   Relates to the ownership of information produced. This includes written documents expressed in a certain way, but can also include other creative formats such as music, artwork or photographs. Copyright is usually held by the creator of a piece of work, but in some cases may be assigned to an employer or university or sold to another third party. Associated copyright law varies from country to country.

Ethics   Systems of moral principles, often thought of as separating right from wrong. They dictate how people lead their lives. Within education, ethical considerations often relate to expected professional conduct and to the wider values of academic integrity.

Plagiarism   When words, information or ideas are taken from a source and used without acknowledgement, this is known as plagiarism. Plagiarism may be deliberate or accidental. Regardless of why this happens, this demonstrates a breach of academic integrity.

Reference list   The list of sources used in an assignment. These are often placed at the end of the assignment. The reference list provides more details about the short citations found in the main body of the text.

Referencing   The process through which the sources of information in an assignment are acknowledged. There are many different referencing systems and each have a slightly different way of presenting the use of sources. Referencing software can be used to support this process.

Self plagiarism   This occurs when you reuse text or ideas from an earlier assignment in a later assignment, without acknowledgement. This would mean that you were trying to get credit for the same work twice.

Source   This refers to the source of words, ideas or other information used in your assignment, if they were not ones that you came up with. Building on existing sources is a core skill of successful academic writing. Sources are acknowledged through correct referencing.

Reference

The Fundamental Values of Academic Integrity:
https://academicintegrity.org/fundamental-values/

Further resources

Here are a range of resources to give you further support in avoiding plagiarism at university.

Source	Details	Where
Cite Your Source	Super Quick Skills book by Phillip C Shon	SAGE Publications
Contract Cheating website	Website run by the author with details about contract cheating	http://contract cheating.com
European Network for Academic Integrity	Group of European institutions and individuals with an interest in academic integrity. Open to student members	https://www. academicintegrity.eu

Source	Details	Where
Find Your Source	Super Quick Skills book by Phillip C Shon	SAGE Publications
International Center for Academic Integrity	An international organisation that promotes academic integrity and supports students and instructors	https:// academicintegrity.org
Plagiarism Today	Website with popular news relating to plagiarism, including the Plagiarism in Pop Culture series	https://www. plagiarismtoday.com/
Take Great Notes	Super Quick Skills book by Mal Leicester and Denise Taylor	SAGE Publications
Thomas Lancaster website	Website of the author, including a blog with many posts covering plagiarism relating issues	http:// thomaslancaster. co.uk